Years at the Ending
Poems 1892–1982

JOSEPH LEFTWICH

Years at the Ending Poems 1892–1982

Cornwall Books

New York • London • Toronto

© 1984 by Rosemont Publishing & Printing Corporation

Cornwall Books
440 Forsgate Drive
Cranbury, NJ 08512

Cornwall Books
25 Sicilian Avenue
London WC1A 2QH, England

Cornwall Books
2133 Royal Windsor Drive, Unit 1
Mississauga, Ont., Canada L5J 1K5

Library of Congress Cataloging in Publication Data

Leftwich, Joseph, 1892–
 Years at the ending.

 I. Title.
PR6023.E288Y4   1983   821'.912   83-45131
ISBN 0-8453-4767-5

Printed in the United States of America

This book is dedicated
to the memory of
Ian Parsons
with love
in the spirit of his own dedication to me
of his splendid book
on Isaac Rosenberg

CONTENTS

PREFACE

Joseph Leftwich completed this anthology in the last months of his long life, recognizing perhaps that he had tarried enough in the flesh and was now ready for representation on earth by a spiritual legacy. Poetry, with its immediacy, its candor, its function of self-analysis, was for him a part of living. And in his poetry the tool and the artifact are one. Process blended with fulfillment; he was not troubled by the conventions imposed upon poetry by the clamor of fashion.

Some of the poems included in this volume speak of time fleeting by, youth replaced by maturity, old generations gone, newer ones on the way, as though Lefty himself constituted a segment of the continuum. "I knew his voice, I heard him singing," he writes of the long-departed Glicenstein, but even a leaf "while it whirls into decay, leaves its imprint where it lay."

Such a man may think of the past with regrets, but without sentimentality. Thus he could span the epochs, the artless beauty of his 'Innocence,' which tells of a quartette of youngsters dreaming a future for themselves in London's East End, revealing the same delicate irony that later found the poet joining the Prophet Elijah in a bus queue.

The poetry was the man, the man a monument among his people, fixed in their perceptions like a Patriarch of old. He encounters us, salutes us with a blessing, and allows us to hurry on.

The death of Joseph Leftwich at the age of ninety, that restless pen stilled at last, was no farewell. Rather, take it as a reassurance, for in this anthology, haunted though it must be by personages from another age, the seeker will find renewal. He left friends in good heart; and literature, touched by his ideals, he left in better shape.

Barnet Litvinoff

INTRODUCTION

I closed my first book of poems, *Along the Years* (Anscombe 1937) with a quotation from Rilke: "One should wait and collect sense and sweetness during a whole lifetime, and if possible a long one—and then, right at the end, one might perhaps be able to write ten lines that were good."

But now approaching my ninetieth birthday, when I may claim to have qualified on the ground of a long life, I find Holbrook Jackson, who stands out in my memory as one of the founders of the *New Age*, telling us that there is a difference between a major poet and a minor. It is not a degree of goodness, he says, good or bad poetry, but of one kind or another of poetry, major and minor themes. To him my poetic technique seemed "a wise balance between the new that is always growing old and the old that is always new."

I stand of course in the shadow of my boyhood friend Isaac Rosenberg, and I have done more than my fair share in getting Rosenberg recognised as a great poet, from the time that a trio of youngsters, Winsten, Rodker and I, decided in 1911 that Rosenberg was a genius.

I did not think at that time that the diary I was keeping would one day become of general interest because of the light it throws on what Rosenberg was doing, or writing. That is why it is now in the Imperial War Museum, with facsimile copies in several other libraries, notably the Whitechapel and Mile End Public Libraries, which we used ourselves.

As Winsten wrote in one of his essays, "Those young people walking round the gloomy, gas-lit streets, talking

11

quietly, laughing, stopping under a lamp-post, while one fumbled in all his pockets for his latest poem."

Gordon Bottomley who, with Denys Harding, did the 1937 Rosenberg *Collected Works*, wrote to me: "Your article about Rosenberg is, of course, valuable for all that you have to tell at first hand of the very early days, with their plain indications of the way he was to take."

I like the way Jean Liddiard, one of the Rosenberg biographers, put it: "Rosenberg and his friends, such as yourself and Winsten, now hold a valued place in the literature of our time."

I think of the poem I wrote when I heard of Rosenberg's death in France, the poem that went by mistake into Edmund Blunden's *Anthology of War Poems*. I treasure Gordon Bottomley's letter to me at the time, about the printer's error that had led to publication as a Rosenberg poem, instead of a dedication to his memory. I treasure it particularly for the closing remark, "I saw some of your other poems in 'Colour,' and thought them very promising." It brought me in a way closer to Rosenberg's whole family, made me accepted as almost an adopted member of the family.

It led also to Jon Silkin writing to me, offering a place on his free list for his poetry magazine *Stand,* "a salute to your sustained contribution to the recognition of Rosenberg." Quite recently the poem appeared again in the *Collected Works,* and Ian Parsons who compiled the book and dedicated it to me included it in the dedication.

I find it of interest that speaking of the group of writers and poets that met at Toynbee Hall, A. B. Levy, in his book *East End Story,* put me at the top of the list of poets, though Rosenberg and Aaronson were in his group. I think too of Charles Landstone's recollection of me as a youngster: "I remember him so well, the young thin poet, and the aristocratic voice that quivered with a poetic passion, especially when he was talking about his beloved Yiddish literature."

We had a lot to do to get Rosenberg recognised. His sister, Annie Wynick, must take first place for her indefatigable efforts on his behalf. F. R. Leavis places the recognition of Rosenberg with the Complete Works, got out by Harding and Bottomley. "Its enrichment of the English language by a dozen pages of great poetry, but also the enrichment of tradition by a new legend. And Rosenberg belongs not with Chatterton, but rather with Keats and Hopkins." There was not even the lack of an undertone of anti-semitism, that made Rosenberg write his poem "Moses," "Then why do They Sneer at Me!"

Rosenberg was not only a Jew. He was also not of the leisured university-educated class to which Sir Arthur Quiller Couch said that nearly all the great English poets of the last century belonged. He reminded us in one of his lectures to the literature students at Cambridge that "The great poets of the last hundred years or so—Coleridge, Wordsworth, Byron, Shelley, Keats, Tennyson, Browning, Rossetti were university men, and Keats was the only one not fairly well-to-do." Again Leavis's conclusion: "Rosenberg belongs with Keats."

Even now, not everybody has yet been reconciled to accepting Rosenberg among our great poets. And Rosenberg too felt his lack of education. There is his letter in the Collected Works: "You mustn't forget the circumstances I had been brought up in, the little education I had. Nobody put poetry in my way."

Others have pointed this out. For instance, Kenneth Allott, who compiled the *Penguin Book of Contemporary Verse:* "I can not on the evidence regard Rosenberg as a major poet. . . . Some writers have looked on him as a poet with promise of greatness. Though I have more sympathy with it than I once had, most writers are agreed that only a few of his poems are completely realised."

This book would not be completed without a word of my part in Yiddish language and literature. I hold dear the things some of our most important Yiddish poets have said about my Yiddish poems. Melech Ravitch, the world traveler, carrying with him a load of poems, his own and others, said "His poems are remarkable; their simplicity is often that of personal comments on the margin of the prayer book. And he makes them more concise, writes

13

them in short lines—short poems filled with honest truth. He knows Yiddish with all its twists and turns, like all of us."

Leyeless, who was for years President of the Yiddish PEN Centre and chief of the introspective movement in Yiddish poetry, In Sich, said: "If I were asked which of his poems made the most direct and also the most intimate impact on me I would point to a group of poems of which 'Meaning' is the best and most representative."

And there is Sutzkever. As Editor of the front-rank Yiddish literary publications, *Di Goldene Keit* (The Golden Chain), talking about our first meeting after the liberation, he wrote: "We met as old friends, fated with word and fire. So it was then, so it was always, in London, in Tel Aviv. To the English writer Leftwich, the Yiddish mother tongue is not an ism, not a step-child. It is a bright light."

I slipped into the habit when I was a youngster of opening a book at random, picking up a sentence and letting it revolve at the back of my mind. I did that the other day with a Mcluhan book, because of a remark there by George Steiner, "When people approached T. S. Eliot and said, 'Mr. Eliot, when you were writing "Sweeny Among the Nightingales," in that passage did you mean . . ,' he would wait patiently and say, 'Yes, I must have meant that if that's what you get out of it.' Eliot was saying that the reader was the poet. It's the reader's job to make poems. The reader is co-poet. The reader's job is to make poems out of the ingredients handed to him."

I think Emerson said something like that. Or Oliver Wendell Holmes in *The Autocrat at the Breakfast Table*. "You stow away some idea and don't want it, say for ten years. When it turns up at last it has got so jammed and crushed out of shape that it is no more like what it was than a raisin is like a grape on the vine."

"We are traveling through the deserts together, like the children of Israel," he concludes. "Some pick up more manna than others."

Some of the manna we pick up on the way is much larger than the rest. Indeed, according to the Rabbis, "the manna was adapted to the taste of the individual—to the

14

adult it tasted like food of the adult, while to the suckling it tasted like the milk of its mother's breasts."

When I started writing just before the First World War it was with an outburst of anti-war screamings. If any of it had survived it would most likely have been, as recently in Chris Searle's anthology of Labour poems, "Bricklight."

In another direction, my Yiddish writing. Or rather, not my own. Someone researching on Isaac Rosenberg came to me not long ago very excited about some reference I had made to Isaac Rosenberg's father writing Yiddish poetry. I had introduced him to some young Yiddish poets in Whitechapel, and he had found them of interest. It had been Isaac Rosenberg's wish that I should translate some of his poems into Yiddish, especially that his father should see what he was trying to say. And I had picked on one of the easier, singing poems, "If You Are Fire." I can still remember the Yiddish words, singing on my tongue. It went together with another Rosenberg poem, "The One Lost," written about the same time. Rosenberg had come to me with the poem new in his mind. He wrote it out for me on the back of an envelope addressed to me. I lent it years later to an American Rosenberg researcher, and I never got it back.

And that brings me to my conclusion now—my quotation, at the outset, from Rilke—"One should wait and collect sense and sweetness during a whole lifetime, and if possible a long one—and then, right at the end, one might perhaps be able to write ten lines that were good."

—Joseph Leftwich, 1982

Years at the Ending
Poems 1892–1982

ISAAC ROSENBERG

I think it was by chance,
By oversight you died in France.
You were so poor an outward man,
So small against your spirit's span,
That Nature, being tired awhile,
Saw but your outward human pile;
And Nature, who would never let
A sun with light still in it set,
Before you even reached your sky,
In inadvertence let you die.

IMMINENCE

Winsten, Rosenberg, Rodker, I,
How we are saddened and broken by
Struggles and teasing hopes and fears.
What awaits us in coming years?
Midnight struck, then one o'clock, two,
We still talked of what things we would do.
Down Hannibal Road, Jamaica Street,
Then back again, with untiring feet,
We talked of our hopes and of our fears.
My own house listened with eager ears.
How much sunk into its brick and wood?
Will it remember how we stood
And graved our names upon the wall?
How much shall we ourselves recall,
In after years, when we shall be
Ripened to maturity.
Life holds us as the nutshell the nut.
What lies outside this shell inshut?

Our crop of thoughts heavy grows,
Too heavy for our young boughs.
Crop? Boughs? We are still only roots.
Who knows if we ever shall grow fruits?
Yet somewhere fruits are, that wait, and know
Where we shall branch for them to grow.

ISAAC ROSENBERG

You stood, a morning star,
At the end of our street.
But your face did not yet shine.
Your halo was not complete.

"Dead Man's Dump" was not yet written.
You had not yet seen soldiers die.
Your question, where had their life gone,
And your own life soon went.
You had not yet asked anyone.

Because you died you live.
Your timber caught fire.
You are ablaze,
A funeral pyre.

ZANGWILL

Someone gathered rich apples, rich corn,
Grown of your heart and your brain,
And in me, as a loft, has stored
Some of the fruit and grain.

The loft smells sweet with its store:
The corn for making bread,
Apples for cider to drink.
And the floor for a weary head.

Though your fields grow no more grain,

And your trees no more apples bear,
Your ripe corn still stands high,
And many reapers are reaping there.

HERZL

How much seed must be sown
Till such another be grown!
So much seed, through the years,
We scattered, and watered with tears.
And there grew tall trees.
But for us little hope in these.
They bent, they split, they broke.
But you were iron-hearted oak.
So we scooped out your living heart;
And we tore the roots apart.

Who knows what such a tree
Might yet have grown to be.
For the few torn strands
Men bear over seas and lands,
And hold to the worshipping view,
As the true parts of you,
How would they have grown through the years,
Being watered by our tears?
How much more seed must be sown
Till such another be grown!

HANS HERZL

One said,
Forget him, now he is dead,
He added, this one,
He was only a great man's futile son.
Poor lad,
His life was sad,
He could not live up to his father's name.
He brought his memory shame.

Now he is dead,
Forget him, he said.

So we praise our great man,
And forget his son.
What this one said,
Says everyone.
But I was Hans Herzl's friend, to me
He was himself, not Herzl's destiny.
He had a heart, and questing mind.
What he sought was of another kind.

The bright light round his father's head
So dazzled him, that he fled.
He wanted a gentler light, more dim.
He stumbled into darkness before darkness came for
    him.
He could not follow his father's deeds and faith,
But he followed him to his early death.
The Jewish land is Herzl's monument.
But his son's heart was broken and rent.

HERZL'S REBURIAL IN JERUSALEM

Once a man looked down from a mountain,
Once the man from the mountain stepped down.
And where he stepped on the mountain side,
He dropped seed, and there grew a town.

"My name is Herzl," the man cried aloud.
"I have come with a dream to you.
If you will, it will be,
The dream will come true.

"Our roots are in this land.
On its soil we shall grow,
Here on the mountain side,
And in the valleys below.

"As King Solomon built in this land God's House,
We will rebuild it here.
You will come to the Temple in Jerusalem,
From far and near."

This man Herzl died far from this land,
Fifty years ago.
Today he came back to the land his dream has built.
The dreamer whose fulfilled dream we see and know.

"The dream is not so different from the act," he said,
"As some folk believe."
All men have done began as a dream.
"I said this day would come when it was the eve."

They welcome him like a father.
All this has sprung from his loins.
Everyone who joins this army,
His army joins.

"On your shoulders we all stand," they tell him.
"We are no longer forsaken.
Our feet have stood firm, because of you,
Though the whole world was shaken.

"The spring you uncovered,
Now swollen with rich rain,
Like a river of healing
Carries to the sea our pain."

The soldiers and the politicians,
The scholars and the ploughmen at the plough,
He dreamed them and dreamed what they are doing,
All they are now.

He holds this land and its people,
Like Moses, on his hands.
Buried, he is the foundation stone
On which everything stands.

Because he dreamed there is now a fortress,
And watchmen on their high tower,
And children, playing and singing,
And trees that are in flower.

"These gates stand because you stood.
Because you dreamed, we are here.
Each dawn lights your memory.
Your Yorzeit flame burns clear."

GLICENSTEIN

I model clay and chisel wood.
People say the work is good.
If I would give my work away,
What a pleasant man, they would say.

But who will fire my clay,
If I cannot pay?
Or cast bronze for me
Without a fee?

The clay goes dry,
And crumbles. I
Fling back the forms I shaped in vain,
Into the unshaped clay again.
And I begin anew,
To model and hew.

Even the logs cost too dear.
What a surly man, say the people here.
They know not how many devils of work
Under my surly eyelids lurk,
That want to be shaping, hewing stone,
And I can give them no blocks to work upon.

So I must model clay, in vain.
To fling back my forms into clay again.

How little he has done, they say, at his age,
And my heart like an earthquake rocks with rage.
Even when I smile, tranquil-faced,
It is like a quiet field with a mine in its bosom placed.

BEETHOVEN

Yesterday Glicenstein finished his statue
Of Beethoven, standing with head bold high,
His hands to his breast, that seems like an organ
Swelling with music. Could such ever die,
Could this man, majestic, triumphant, die?
Like iron girders, the lines of him, upright,
Like furrows deep-driven and straight, they lie.
On the girders a mighty edifice builded,
In the furrows the ripe seed springing high.
All that is builded, all that is planted,
Undying, lasting, strong.
A glance, a touch, and all around it
Bursts into exultant song.
Can song vanish, will music fly?
This Titan who sends forth the hurricane.
Could he lose his power, relinquish, die?

To-day, as he came through New Oxford Street,
Glicenstein brought from Mudies' Beethoven's death
    mask,
And all day he stood at his newer task,
Put it on canvas, painted it ghostly grey-green,
The flat face overlaid with sorrow and pain,
Holes where his eyes were that have death seen.
This dead man could live, could die, has died.
Here is not music, but a suffering man,
Who had dropsy, was deaf, embittered, cried,
And out of his cries made tremendous music,
Out of the depths a splendour of song.
Shattered, like Job, he praised his victor.
Defeated, he gave exultant tongue.

That other, unhumbled, proud head held high,
Is no man, but a demon, a spirit, a storm,
Could never have lived, for he could never die.

THE GLICENSTEIN MUSEUM

I knew his voice. I heard him singing
A song he sang to me in London thirty years ago,
About the Emperor who had so many clothes
He spent all day putting on and off.
Here in Safad I heard him sing this song,
In the Hamsin heat, in the midst of the crowd,
I heard him. The others heard speakers praise him.
I heard him sing.

That night, in the cool moonlight
All Safad sang to us,
Her narrow, steep streets
That we walked like rope-ladders
Sang to us the song of the Cabbalists.
The shadows walking with us under the moon were
    shades,
Joseph Caro, who wrote his Shulchan Aruch in Safad,
Isaac Luria and Chaim Vital
Whose words resounded in Polish Yeshibas;
They wrote them in Safad.

Glicenstein walked with us.
A shade with those shades.
Did they descend with him, with us
To the studios of the artists of Safad,
Where we sat all night,
Laughing, talking, singing?
Glicenstein was with us.
He is with both.
Yeshiba student and artist, both.
I saw him look at the paintings on the easels.
I heard him join our songs.

As dawn came over the hills of Safad,
Glicenstein walked back with us.
We passed the Glicenstein Museum as the sun rose.
His son was singing;
But Glicenstein did not join his song.
His phantom-shape was silent.
He was exalted, like a King.
In the glow of the sunrise in Safad
I saw a golden crown upon his head.

MY FRIENDS

John, John,
Rodker John,
I think of days that long have gone.
Rosenberg and Winsten, you,
Dreamed with me of things we'd do!
Rosenberg is dead, the War
Silenced him. He sings no more.
And many now his loss deplore
Who would not heed his song before.

You and Winsten both are bald,
Though burning memories still scald.
While I with hair still long, am grey;
Youth and dreams have gone away.
You have children, Winsten, you,
What you hoped they still may do.
I have lost my parents, ground
Under me. And have not found
That new hold by which men live,
The hope renewed that children give.
Do your children give, indeed,
What I the childless lack and need?

John, John,
Rodker John,
What have we the dreamers done?

We have toiled and earned our bread,
We have loved and we have wed,
We have written poems, too,
Were and are a crazy crew.

Twenty years ago and more
We were friends, before the War.
Rosenberg is dead and sainted.
We three left were once acquainted.

ZUTPHEN

Birth is my greatest happening,
Yet I remember it not.
Nor do I recognise this place,
Though I was born on this spot,
Though the midwife remembers well,
Who here beside me stands.
She knows when I came from the womb,
She received me on her hands.
I was an infant when from here
My parents took me away.
For twenty years I have not seen
Zutphen, until this day.
Yet always, at school in England,
I read the tale with pride,
Of how Sir Philip Sidney
Here in my Zutphen died.

SIR PHILIP SIDNEY

What can I say to you,
As together we stride?
I know here, where I was born,
Only you who here died.

The air bends to my thought.
The ground rises to my desire.

There is trumpeting round me,
And the sound of musket fire.

Here, from a trench,
Came the musket shot
That wounded you.
You died near this spot.

Here your last minute
Met my first.
You died on this ground
Where I was nursed.

"Love my memory," you said
To those near when you died.
I was not yet born,
But I heard what you cried.

The cup of water
You gave here to another.
Refreshed me often,
Made me love you, brother.

The years dip down,
Your years meet mine.
Here in Zutphen
They are one line.

"In this small course," you sang,
"Which birth draws out to death."
We meet, I, the living,
With you, the wraith.

You, the brave knight,
I the Whitechapel Jew,
Who in my Whitechapel school
Gloried in you.

I am an oldish man now.
White-haired, dim-eyed,

Twice as old as you were,
When here you died.

Your shade stretches
Over to me,
I, still living.
You, history.

A little longer,
And I shall, too,
Lie in Abraham's bosom,
As you do.

Your day and mine
Will then be one.
But the Yssel will still
Through our Zutphen run.

IN A BOMB SHATTERED HOUSE

Are you here, my father and mother,
Are you here in this house where you died,
Where you lay on your bier, on this floorboard,
I, mourning at your side?

In this empty house, with shattered windows,
In this house where the walls will soon crash,
I pass my fingers where no hold is,
Over the crumbling sill and rotting sash.

My thoughts of you are more solid
Than this crumbling wall.
When they have pulled down this ruined brickwork,
I shall still hear you call.

REGINALD GATENBY
My Schoolmaster

I shape my letters as you shaped them.
I speak my words as you used to do.

Your line of Lincoln Englishry
Went deep into this Whitechapel Jew.

My Yiddish and Hebrew, my Jewishness,
Are the firm foot on which I stand.
But you made me also native here,
At home in our English land.

I speak English words as you spoke them.
I write them as you wrote.
This Whitechapel Jew has his mind full
Of your English thought.

IN THE TUBE
For Victor Lewisohn

I suppose they are laughing at me, some of them,
    And some are wondering whether I am mad,
Because I stand here holding to the strap,
    And mumble to myself, and seem absorbed and sad.
They see my lips are moving, and they fear
    I am insane, and talking to myself of madmen's
        dreams.
How should they know I am praying here,
    Because it is the time for Mincha—Twilight Prayer,
Before the sun goes down? The sun is setting now,
    It will be dusk before I leave the train;
So in the train I speak with God.
    Let them look on and think I am insane—
I thank God! I utter the old Hebrew prayer,
    And half the time I cannot see these folk for thoughts
        of God.

A PRAYER
For A. A. Wolmark

God, in painting my life,
Use colours that are rich:
Do not scrape them with the palette-knife,

31

To make them smooth and thin. I care not which
You use of all Your colours, red or gold,
Purple or black, so that they stand out bold,
Not lost in muddy grey;
Fill me with joy, or else with sorrows pack;
Paint as You will, but this I pray:
Use colour, even if it is Your deepest black.

JABOTINSKY

This was a tongue that like a hammer fell,
And where it struck beat hearts to steel,
Steel from which swords are made,
To liberate those enslaved and betrayed.
Iron and steel, weapons strong
He wrought, hammering with his tongue.

Speak to the Children of Israel,
Cried that voice that like a hammer fell.
Give up for iron and for steel
All you hold precious, wealth and weal,
Flocks and oil and wine and wheat,
Take iron, and arms and armour beat.

So that tongue like a hammer fell and beat
Against many anvils, in furnace heat,
Unresting, unsparing, till blow after blow
A crack widened, and spread right through.
The tongue that like a hammer fell,
Now is silent, now lies still.

ABRAHAMS

Whitechapel was your tongue,
Jerusalem your heart.
You lie dead where your heart took you.
You live in your English song.

Whitechapel taught us English.
You were like Rosenberg to me.
You gave your life for Zion.
But left English Poetry.

You came a singing bird,
From a Whitechapel slum,
As Zangwill and Rosenberg came,
As I come.

God denied you the length of days
For which you prayed.
But while He left you with us,
You sang as He bade.

Now you are smitten with silence.
The curtain is drawn about your head.
But your songs have not departed.
We still hear what you said.

Your tools were pen and paper.
You fought with tongue and sword.
Now your tools and your weapons
Are laid up with the Lord.

JOAN

How shall I tell
What you are to me?
If I am the singer,
You are the melody.

If I sing
In a sad strain,
I am the grief,
Because you are the pain.

If the wild wind
Blows down my roof,

To rebuild your house
My frame is enough.

Under your firm flesh,
My daughter Joan,
I uphold you,
The bone.

JOY

Joy wears a white frock,
And a white ribbon in her hair.
She wears white shoes,
And hugs a teddy bear.

Joy has a child's happy smile,
And laughing voice,
She puts her eager hand in mine.
And makes me rejoice.

Joy is ten years old,
My singing one,
Among a crowd of laughing children,
My Joan.

SINGING TO JOAN

I am singing to you, Joan.
Though my words mean nothing to you yet,
You will grow to know my voice,
A sound of love you will not forget.

If the words mean nothing to you,
You will grow to know the sounds,
Full of liquid l's for love,
And rich r's that ring their rounds,

Baby b's and cradling k's,

Sweet s's soothing you to sleep,
Velvet v's like the wings of doves,
And p's with which to plant and reap.

Seed and springing fruit, my child,
Crop and harvest of my life.
All your mother and I have been,
Mystic mating of man and wife.

Magic m's for your mother's arms.
When you grow to womanhood,
You will remember these singing sounds,
Before the words were understood.

MY DAUGHTER

Not I have shaped you, not I, although
Flesh of my flesh and bone of my bone,
My child, my daughter, my Joan, my Joan;
Flesh of my flesh and blood of my blood,
Dear witness of my proud fatherhood,
Not I have shaped you and made you grow,
Though of me and your mother shaped and grown,
Our child, our daughter, our Joan, our Joan.

How often, how often we desired
Child of our flesh and bone of our bone;
But no will of ours could shape you, Joan—
Not our will, not joy, not grief, not pain;
Through hungry years we desired in vain.
Till when hope had drooped and ardour tired,
Of your mother and me shaped and grown,
The good God made you, our Joan, our Joan.

PORTRAIT BUST

Joan's seeking fingers
Run over plane and line,

The tumbled hair, and the face muscles
Of this young face that was mine.

Before she was born,
Dead Glicenstein she never knew,
Modelled this likeness of me,
From whose loins she grew.

She will remember her father,
When I am dead,
Not as she knows me now,
But by this youthful head.

Here am I, as I shall be
For my child's children to see.
As Glicenstein shaped me I shall live
When I am in my grave.

PROPHECY

When I was a child, my father lifted me on his shoulder,
And strode with long striding steps along country roads,
Carrying me swiftly on his strong shoulder.
That is how I often remember my father—
Long-legged, young, carrying me along country roads,

Now he is dead, and I knew him old and ill,
I like to think of my father as a young man, carrying me
    on his strong shoulder along country roads.

I am an oldish man of fifty,
And I have a small child of my own.
I sometimes lift her on my shoulder.
But she has strong, sturdy legs, my Joan;
She walks sturdily at my side for miles,
Through London streets, along country roads,
Prattling, laughing singing as she is walking,
Holding my hand as she walks sturdily by my side.

And though I am an oldish man of fifty,
I thank God I can see
Joan walking by my side, sturdily,
And I thank God I can hear
Joan laughing and singing and prattling at my side.

Sing Joan, sing!
Our world is black, and we old ones are old.
But before he died,
My friend Stefan Zweig prophesied—
Leftwich, our world has bungled, and our life is harder
    than I want to bear.
But your daughter will live
To see a better world and breathe freer air.

PRAYERS

Prayers are words,
Liturgy.
Millions said these prayers
Before me.
The Psalms David wrote
We repeat.
We speak his bitterness,
And his sweet.

Comfort ye, comfort ye,
The Prophet said.
His words long ago
Today I read.
I cry each morning,
"God is One."
Each night before I sleep,
"God's will be done."

The words Moses spoke
Are on my lips.
And in the Tephilin on my head,

And on my arm and finger tips.
To the God of Abraham, Isaac and Jacob
I offer their prayer.
In their words I thank Him
For removing my despair.

They left me a heritage
Of their words and song.
They fitted them to my mind,
And to my tongue.
Their words that are on my lips,
Have coursed through my heart,
They are part of me now,
Of my spirit part.

With my reins and my tongue
Their praises I sing.
I bless with their words
The Lord God, our King.
They trod out the road for me,
With their prayer.
I shall not lose my way now,
Following them there.

RODKER
"It's always very exciting when a new life is born"
Letter from John Rodker when my daughter was born.

When we were young we sought to know
Where we would branch, for our fruit to grow.
Now you are dead we know well
What fruit you bore before you fell.

Rosenberg died long ago.
His rich fruit many know.
Four young trees grew in Stepney Green.
Two were cut down; two remain.

Winsten and I who were young with you
Bow our heads, as old folk do.

We know now how we four
Branched, and what fruit we bore.
The signs I now seek to read
Are, how grows my seed.

THE WINDS WILL HEAR

Words are trees,
Branching sound,
Speech rooted
In the ground.

Some speech is oak.
Mine is willow-tree.
The waters of Babylon
Speak here to me.

From far away
Come these winds that blow.
My father heard them
Long ago.

A singing log,
He was cut down.
But his words in me
Have become my own.

New sap rises
To my head.
His voice still speaks,
Though he is dead.

When I am felled,
Like a log lie,

My child will spread
Her branches high.

And the winds will hear
Her lift her voice.
And I, though dead,
Will rejoice.

MY MOTHER

My mother sits in heaven waiting for my coming.
"He will be tired after all that way.
I must have the place ready for his arrival.
There will be so much for us to say."

My mother used to sit like that, waiting
Every Sabbath eve for me to come,
To welcome the Sabbath with her.
To say Kiddush in her home.

My mother has eyes as blue
As the blue heaven where she sits.
While my mother waits for my coming,
She has a sock in her hand that she knits.

"He will be tired after so much walking.
He must wash his feet and change his socks,
Before he says Kiddush at the Sabbath feast,
With roast Leviathan and Great Ox."

My mother's hair is silver as sunlight.
In my mother's eye hangs a silvery tear.
My mother weeps with joy in heaven—
"My son will soon be here."

MY FATHER

My father is sunlight
On the page of my book.

His bearded face is in the letters.
The words I read have his look.

His firm handgrip holds me.
Sunlight is in my eyes.
My father who begot me,
Reminds me a man dies.

I put down my book.
I hold fast to his hand.
My father leads me
To his new land.

Sunlight casts shadows.
But shadows are there
Only when the sun shines.
Without sun they disappear.

My eye holds my father.
My lips repeat his thought.
I am the shadow
His sunlight brought.

I am shadow in my room.
He is sunlight on my book.
The letters have his features.
The words have his look.

THE SUN IS IN MY EYES

The sun is in my eyes.
My eyeballs are aflame.
In letters of fire
I spell out God's Name.

The sun is in my eyes.
Burnt up is my tongue.
But deep down in my heart
Still rises my song.

41

The song rises in me,
Though I cannot see.
I know there is light,
All round me.

That was Elijah
Who gripped my hand.
I am an old man, I told him.
I can hardly stand.

I am older, Elijah answered.
You have another three years to go,
Before you are like me an old Jew.

The sun has moved on.
The glow has abated.
I have been visited,
And dated.

I have three more years, said Elijah.
Three more years under the sun,
Then I shall lie underground.
And my journey will be done.

ELIJAH ERRED

Elijah erred, or I misheard.
He said in three years I will be dead.
Six years have gone, and I am still alive!
But how could Elijah have erred?
How could I have mistaken his word!

I saw Elijah standing at this bus stop.
And I was dog-tired, ready to drop.
I told him that much, as I joined his queue.
One old Jew to another old Jew.

You think you are old, Elijah said,
But I am older,

And he laid his head like a friend on my shoulder.

Is it right, God, that Elijah should be wrong?
Who dictated the wrong words to his tongue?
But better I should have misheard,
Better than that Elijah should have erred!

DEATH IS NOT STRANGE

Death is not strange.
Strange is life,
That flesh can think,
And body believe,

That dust can sing;
That a clod
For a man's lifetime
Can house God.

That dead things live
When touched by God's breath,
Is the miracle,
Not death.

How the silence leans
Against each stone.
The dead lie together,
Yet alone.

My mother's great-aunt,
Who lies here,
Lived one hundred
And ten year.

Through all those years dying,
Till she was as dead
As her young-died brother,
Of whom she said,

Looking on me—
"My brother's great-grandson!"
Now both are dead,
Is it all one?

Often my lips chilled
On that parched leathern face,
So much death had already
Lodged in that space.

Is it all one,
That in a dead town,
This was an ancient palace
Before it crashed down?

MY DEAD

Today I shall count my dead,
The lives that my lifestream fed,
That poured their waters into me,
Till a high river now I be,
While far away their own source dried,
And they no longer are, have died.
What of their waters now in me,
Without which I would no high river be?
In other streams, too, their waters flow,
As mine into many streams shall go.

My parents' water flow most in me.
Though who shall say whose each drop be?
And many waters in me flow
From streams whose names I do not know,
That on through stream to stream have gone,
That a few drops in me may run,
Though they as streams have long gone dry.
Yet once all streams were one,
As all mankind when Adam was alone,
And we all stood at Sinai.

Then from the fire the living waters flowed,
When God upon the mountain stood,
Round about, the whole earth glowed,
Almost melting into flood.
So many sparks from one great fire,
Begotten by the single Sire.
Fire to water, water, blood,
Lo, all the Lord has done is good.
The streams of life flow on.
Life is never done.

THE SUN

The sun came strolling down our street,
Over the roofs on hands and feet,
Over the roofs, till it came to our church,
And knocked the weathercock off its perch.
Then it tried to climb over, but the spire at the top
Was so sharp that it tickled, and the sun had to stop
To laugh. And the spike of the steeple stuck it through.
Our church had the sun itself on view.

Ten thousand people came to see.
They thought it a pity the sun should be
Stuck up on a spike. But it looked fine,
It went to my head like wine.
It went to my head; I shouted with glee,
I laughed at the sun that it couldn't get free.

I laughed at the sun, but I didn't laugh long.
It suddenly struck me laughing was wrong.
The sun should be going about, giving light,
Not stuck on a steeple. The people were right,
The people who wanted the sun to be free.
The sun should be freed. And freed by me.

I took off my coat and prepared for the climb.
The crowd had been sullen all the time.

Now it applauded. I thought it meant me,
Then I looked up, and the sun, I could see,
Had slipped off the spike, without waiting for me.

SOLOMON'S SON

Wisdom is not in the schools,
But in the wise!
And you read it not in their books,
But in their eyes.
You cannot put wisdom on
With the robes of Solomon.
Why, so did King Rehoboam,
Who was wise Solomon's son,
And sat on his magic throne,
Yet he brought about Israel's doom.
He rent the kingdom in twain,
That was never united again,
And no man now can tell
Where are the lost tribes of Israel.
Not enough are the robes of the wise,
Nor their thrones nor their books,
Nor even their blood.
King Solomon's son
With his robes put foolishness on.

EGYPT

This was Sahara I flicked from my shoe.
I walked in Sahara to-day,
As a swimmer comes wet from the sea,
I came sand-flecked away.
What else have I brought from Sahara's edge?
Tired face and weary eyes.
I saw the Sphinx with no astonishment.
The Pyramids with no surprise.
What the Sphinx to one who comes new might tell,

Museum Sphinxes had told.
Must we who know the Pyramid shape,
Pilgrim to its matrix-mould?

But I had come flying to Egypt!
Looking down had seen clouds below!
What marvel after such marvel
Could the Pyramids show?
And I came through the Tyrol,
Where the peaks rise up sheer!
How puny beside God's Pyramids
Are these men-built Pyramids here!
Not more than the specks of sand my shoe
Brought from the desert back,
Besides Sahara's vast
Immovable track.

LIFE

If a bird sings on my branches,
Is it I, the tree, who sings?
No! For I, the tree, am weeping,
Weeping to God for wings.
I, the tree, have no voice for singing.
And I could sing such wondrous things.

THE YEARS

And all the years of suffering,
Of suffering and pain,
Are as the words the poet writes,
And crosses out again.

And all the years of happiness,
Of happiness that throng,
Are as the words of loveliness
That go to make a song.

EVEN A LEAF

Even a leaf that has lain
Close to the ground in the rain,
Being blown off by the wind,
Leaves its impression behind,
Leaves its imprint on the ground
While it whirls wind-driven round,
While it whirls into decay
Leaves its imprint where it lay.

HOSPITALITY

Let my house be open wide,
To the east and to the west,
To the north and to the south,
Let who will, come be my guest.

He may come from west or east,
From north or south to share my feast.
He may sit at ease and rest,
And when he please
He may go forth,
To east or west,
To south or north.

THE CANDLE

They say that yonder tiny star
Is vaster than our world, and all we are.
And yet that mighty ball in space
Sheds but a feeble light upon your face.

It is a miser, tremblingly
Hoarding its light to last eternity.

How better is this candle, joyously

Burning its heart out in a blaze,
Knowing no stint, and like a song of praise
Going into the dark exultingly.

SMITTEN

Blessed are the smitten,
Happy are the blows,
When Moses holds up his staff,
And we huddle to him close.

Blessed are the smitten,
When Moses smites the rock,
And the water comes gushing out,
Water for our flock.

Blessed are the stricken,
Happy are the blows,
When God holds you close to him,
Lovingly close.

STANDING AT MY GRAVE

Here, where I stand now,
When I am dead I shall lie below.
On this spot,
My plot,
All my busy-business done,
Here in my grave my own, my one,
Numbered and paid for,
With my name on the headstone,
Like the brass plate on my front door.
Here I shall lie, waiting for my call.
Merciful God, Your Voice calls everywhere,
And I, good God, I am deaf! I cannot hear!

GALBANUM

He must be a happy man, they say,
Praying his Thanksgiving to God, each day.
He must have much to thank God for.
He hopes God will give him more.
So he offers incense, sweet herbs, spices,
Hymns of praise and sacrifices.

But God knows how with the spikenard and the myrrh
So much bitterness is mingled there—
With each weight of balsam and sweet gum.
I have my due part of bitter galbanum.

My bitter grief brings my spirit close—
Seeking comfort, Lord, to your Mercy Seat.
I come to You with my naked woes.
I add no honey to make it seem sweet.

WORDS

Where I sit at my table,
Holding my pen,
Setting down letter by letter
Words to be read by men,

The words are not of my making.
God made all the tongues.
But I must now finish the words that fit together
To make the meaning to which word belongs.

I have been told to convey the message,
Which others have conveyed before me.
The words form as I write them
With whatever the message may be.

So I sit here at my table,
Holding my pen,
Setting down letter by letter,
The message to be read by men.

50

LETTERS

Hold on to those letters.
Watch their different shapes,
How they twist into meaning.
Till the word escapes.

They are lamps, these letters.
Hung at the gate
By which we enter,
Illuminate.

And their light sings
Into the air,
A psalm of thanksgiving,
A hymn, a prayer.

Hold on to those letters.
When they leave your Ark,
They form a disturbing
Question mark,

Like Jonah's cry,
Like Job's despair,
Like the agony Saul
Found too much to bear.

Hold on to that A,
Lest it joins the B,
And brings thought of your father,
Memory.

Turn it towards N.
And to the letter I,
That the three together
Yourself signify.

Probe your own meaning,
Word by Word,
Letter by letter,
Dimmed and blurred

With tears that your father
Left on your page,
And the marginal notes
He wrote on your edge.

MEANING

These are strange words I utter,
Unclear characters I write.
Incomprehensible sounds I mutter.
I cannot understand them quite.

There is a meaning that will bind them together,
If I can find where it is hid.
I cannot know while I am seeking, whether
It will empower or forbid.

Yet somewhere among the sounds I utter,
Among the syllables I am writing here,
Is a word that will form with a hesitant stutter,
And then the meaning will be clear.

Then all I have been writing and saying
Will fall into place, and fit.
And that for which I am praying,
Fulfilment will come to it.

Among the meaningless jumble,
The struggling discord of sound,
Surefooted, where now I stumble,
My meaning will be found.

COLON

Fifty years I am spelling out letters,
Writing slowly word by word.
The first letters were clumsy and awkward.
Some of the later are blurred.

Yet here is one that has a fine flourish.
And this is a lovely outline.

The commas are in their proper places.
So is my possessive sign.
The sentence is taking shape and meaning.
Yet still I cannot understand
What this is I am writing to dictation,
Now in a very clerky hand.

Fifty years I have been tracing letters,
Writing words down one by one.
Shall I have time to complete a sentence,
And put a full stop when I have done?
But here I set down a colon.
There is something more to be said.
I think I am writing a long sentence
For whoever will read.

BEYOND THE COLON

I have now passed beyond the colon,
And my hand still writes.
The sentence is growing longer,
Through my days and nights.

God grant I may finish my sentence
Before my pen will drop,
That I may complete what I am writing,
And myself set the full stop.

How did my sentence begin?
With an uncertain blob at my birth,
And some ill-fashioned scrawls as I grew—
Nothing of worth.

Is there now any worth in the sentence
I have written down?
What have I said with all these consonants and vowels

That is my own?

That when I am called for examination
At the judgment of my years,
And the Angel tells me to repeat my sentence,
And the host of heaven hears—

I may speak up—all the long sentence I have written,
All my words memorised,
All that in my life has been of value,
All I have loved and prized.

Let my hand not now tremble and falter,
Let my life reach its goal,
That my sentence may be completed—
That my life be whole.

SONG FOR HANNA

Grandfathers are old men
With beards long and grey.
I have become a grandfather, beardless,
But as old as they.

How shall I measure my years now?
Till you came
I counted them one by one.
It is no longer the same.

Now my years are not only counted,
Written on the slate.
Now I must add your little body
To my weight.

When I think of you I say a prayer,
As when your mother was born, my Joan,
Thanking God my flesh and blood will be here,
When I am gone.

My years will still have measuring.
My years will still have weight.
You with your continuing life
My years will consecrate.

One day, Hanna, if I live,
You will clamber on my knee.
And in later years you will remember
And talk about me.

You will tell how your grandfather
Was a man whose life was to write,
And when you were born I wrote a poem,
How you added to my life your weight.

I said you added weight to my living—
To be a grandfather is grand, Hanna!
You will after me sing my Hallelujah!
You will sing my Hosannah!

EQUILIBRIUM

Your tiny weight, Hanna,
Your tiny weight
Restores my balance,
Helps me walk straight.

I had been walking
With a list of late,
Tilted to one side—
An awkward gait.

When your weight struck me,
It righted my feet.
I walk steadily now
Through the street.

As though a plummet were sunk

Deep into me,
I walk like a swimmer who knows
How to battle the sea.

You are, new-born Hanna,
To me a plumb.
When you came I regained
Equilibrium.

LIKE GOOD FRUIT

You are as long as my arm—
The whole length of you.
Yet longer than all my long years,
From which you grew.

Where did my years begin?
In Paradise,
With Adam and Eve,
With the first sunrise.

And the years will, through you, go on
In this earthly clime,
Until the last sunset,
At the end of time.

Through you my seed will spread,
Like in the desert manna,
Like the sweet water at Mara,
Like good fruit, Hanna.

HANNA

How much of me is in you, Hanna?
Your mother's nose, your father's chin.
The arch of your foot, they say is mine—
Your grandmother's hair and skin.

Compounded of us all, you are
Your self heart and soul.
Our different parts have come together
To make your whole.

Our past that has flowed into you,
And your future, what you will be,
Carry you into the years to come,
Shaping your progeny.

Where, Hanna, did your name come from?
"There was a certain man," and his wife, Hanna, prayed.
And in answer to her prayer, Samuel was born—
When you move, Hanna, I hear Samuel's tread.

THE HEIR

It was warm summer when my grandchild was born.
She had a warm coming into our world. And there,
Waiting, was the long line of her ancestors,
Welcoming my grandchild, to us all our heir.

Nothing is greater than this—the line continuing.
From the Creation onward, we go on.
We all, our line from the beginning,
Till you came, Hanna, we are one.

In you our souls are mingled.
In you we all live again.
Where we end, Hannah, with your coming,
We once more begin.

MY TALLITH

For fifty years, when I prayed,
I wore a small prayer-shawl.
I wore it like a silk scarf,
It was so small.

57

Now I am an old man,
I wear a Tallith down to my knees,
A long flowing woollen robe,
With long fringes, and embroideries.

It is the garb my ancestors wore,
When they stood at Mount Sinai.
And heard God, in thunder,
The Decalogue cry.

When I wrap it round me,
I am one of them.
I press it against my eyes, and my heart,
And kiss the fringes on its hem.

I see the Voice that stands
Above them all.
I bow my head, worshipping,
Under my long prayer-shawl.

I wrap my head in my Tallith,
I cover my eyes,
I think how a man lives,
And how a man dies.

I finger the long woollen Tallith,
And think, when I die,
They will wrap my body in it,
The robe in which I shall lie.

KORIM

I lay full length to-day,
On the Synagogue floor,
Prostrate before You,
To bless and adore.

But now I stand,
As You made me, straight.

We walk before You,
We stand and wait.

When we lie down,
And bend our head,
Lord God, we pray,
Raise us from the dead.

THOUGHT

Thought is a tall tree,
Lifting its arms to the night,
On its branch a flower buds,
To burst with the sun into light.

I have grown a thought,
That my hand obeys.
Like a branch to the wind,
It bends and sways.

It sways to the wind,
Like water to the moon.
But I turn to the east,
Where the sun will come soon.

GEBAH

Here are acres
Of rich grain,
In a fabulous
Phantom Plain.
Living men
Sow and reap,
Where the great ghosts
Vigil keep.

Here you may, dimly hearkening,
Still hear triumphant Deborah sing.

I have drunk water, piped and tapped,
From which Gideon's army lapped,
And walked with firm and happy tread
Where Saul called Samuel from the dead.
Children play and old men rest
On Megiddo's warrior breast.
I ate oranges today
That grew where Naboth's vineyard lay.
And I may, striding through the night,
Meet here Elijah, the Tishbite.
Or a sudden thud may tell
Where they threw down Jezebel,
Or the thunder of a wheel,
Jehu speeding
Through Jezreel.

History has eyes,
That watch me here.
The past has come
Very near.
God himself
Through Jezreel goes.
For "Jezreel" means
"The Lord God Sows."

I walked across to Ezekiel,
To the Synagogue of Jezreel,
To keep the God-appointed tryst,
On this Tabernacles feast.
And standing by the scroll, I read:
"The land shall be inhabited.
From Gebah to Rimmon, all the plain
Shall be lifted up again.
From the king's winepress to Hananel,
Here men in the land shall dwell."
God has sown Jezreel, once more,
With men for His threshing floor.
Go, spy out the land,
See, how sturdily they stand,
Ripening acres of rich grain

In this fabulous
Phantom Plain.

YIDDISH

Yiddish is not dead,
To wear a shroud
A garment we never again change,
From foot to head.

Yiddish lives,
She changes her dress.
She adds bright bonnets
To her loveliness.

When she came to the Rhine,
In her Hebrew robes,
She put on German garments.
But she was divine,

For against her skin
God's word she wore,
The Hebrew Torah,
The Hebrew lore.

When from the Rhine
She went to Russian lands,
She picked up finery there,
With eager hands.

In her American travels
She found new frocks,
And new adornments
For her locks.

She took off her Shaitel,
And her big Russian shawl.
She wears a new hat in the spring,
And another in the fall.

She wants to feel
She is at home,
In every place
Where she may come.

She is Mother Yiddish,
No foolish young bride.
She can choose what she wants,
And she can decide

What she should wear,
That suits her best.
She selects what she wants
From whatever is there.

KADDISH

Yisgadal, ve-yiskadash,
Praise God for peace—and hush,
My mother lies beneath the loam,
Asleep in her eternal home.
Her body moulders in the mould.
But all earth, clod by clod, lives, souled
By God's breath passing through, just through.
So long last life—then earthed again, I-you.

In the first man God breathed one living breath,
That still in us comes, goes, is life, is death.
God had not meant that man should die.
So when he fell, life came to you and I,
Into each particle of earth—in, out—
Our lives as quickly pass as thought.
When each earth-particle has lived, will God
Requicken all of us, all earth, each clod?

Then shall earth stand up in the way,
And clap its hands that Resurrection Day.
Behold, the Lord our God is One,
There is nought else but what His thought has done.

He is the atom and the whole vast globe,
All that we probe for, the prober and the probe,
The field of search, the searcher and the found,
The new-born babe, the dead beneath the mound.

What if we die and crumble into earth?
Was not our life the living worth,
If we were clay, and in us God has dwelt,
If clay has known God-knowing, God-like felt.
If clay knew clay, clod loved, communed with clod,
And for a glorious moment drank a toast to God,
Because the clay again is clay,
Would you have rather never known the day?

For is one day not like all other days?
Each morn creation is renewed by God, always.
What we see others have already seen;
What we are others have already been;
Knew the same day, and the same night;
And after us, the same darkness and the same light
That we know now, posterity will know,
As long as life shall come and go.

Different days, yet all the same.
For all from the same Creator came.
How could they different be,
Since He is all, and all is He.
And all the infinite variety
Unites into one Unity?
Only the same day and the same night,
To the new-born give fresh delight.

So, mother, you have lived your day.
Your life-breath rushed out quickly from your clay,
As if there were a sudden break or rent,
Through which with gasping speed it went.
God made in us tubes, vessels, openings, and
If one of them is blocked, or breaks, we cannot stand.
In some the life blood oozes, seeps away,
So slowly that they totter into clay.

In them there is so little living left,
That though they move and speak they seem of life
  bereft;
Another look, another word shall drain
What little store of life may still remain.
You see the life evaporating through their skin,
Slowly, so slowly till there is no more within.
But you stood upright, smiling happily, content,
And at one rush life from you went.

Now you lie cold beneath the mould,
As dead as those who died of old.
One day is as a thousand years in death.
You who were palpable are now a wraith.
And when I feel you snuggle to my heart, and stroke my
  hair
As you loved doing—I fling out my arms, and nothing
  there.

Though the trees shall yield no fruit,
The fields lie bare, and dead each root,
Though God in anger the nations thresh,
And stricken sore is every flesh,
Though God slay, in Him I trust.
He will again raise me from the dust.
Though my mother lies in death.
She will praise God with my breath.

How, if we were one breath, you, I,
Were we together? Must not one first die
Before the breath pass on? But we did share—
Since one God-breath is all life, everywhere.
For life other than God is none.
In His Unity all are one.
We, the atoms of His life-giving breath
Group and re-group. Change of place we call death.
Mother, where breathes your spirit now?
How shall I find you, mother, how?

Under the ground my mother lies—hush.
But God lives! Yisgadal, ve-yiskadash!

YISKOR

Are we the dead whose sons we be?
My father living for a while in me?
One life, from the Creation, lived in parts,
Till the last day—one life in several hearts.
One single breath that Adam had from God,
One breath all life, and all mankind one clod.

We are loaned the spirit for a day,
Then we crumble back to clay.
Yet what we felt and what we were,
Will never from God's memory stir.
For what we aimed at, what we wrought,
Was our clay moving to God's thought.

Lo, all these names the Cantor read,
The dead who bore them are no longer dead.
They throng the synagogue, among us stand.
My father! Let me touch your hand!
I see you, let me feel you too.
Or must I first be dead, like you?

Do I see you, or see a memory in me?
For living people, too, like this I see.
All things we see in the mind remain,
At wish—and unwished, too—are seen again.
If I see living people like this, too,
Do I see memory now, or you?

I have your tephilin, and each tephilin-day
I wear them, as you wore them once, to pray.
Upon my arm and on my head
I set them as a seal with you, the dead.
Your tephilin against my head and brain,
Tingle to your touch again.

Bend nearer. Let me feel your touch,
Your firm hand-grip, tenacious clutch.
Tenacious hands and lips firm-set,
These marked your spirit, mark you yet.

Near, for I see you. Yet too far
To hold you where the living are.

Life, death—above clay, below sod,
One we, live, dead—as we encounter God.
And He who made the flint as water flow,
Can turn the reaper into hoe.
Dead father—I, your living son,
Your reaping and my planting, it is one.

Behold, the wheels seen once by Ezekiel!
Our life is as it were a wheel within a wheel.
One life—when you are lifted up on high,
The spirit for a while is I,
The wheel is lifted or descends,
My time of life begins and ends.

My time of life—but where there is no time,
There is no change, succession, climb
From you to me, and on through space,
But you and I—you-I—for ever in one place.
Eternally as now. Even the clod
A thought-projection is of God.

Yiskor. By God remembered be,
Bound in the bond of life, eternally.

VIDDUI

Bend down Lord, and hear me
Confess my sins to You.
Though You know everything I did,
Better than I do.

I do not need to remind You,
But before I depart,
I must pay my reckoning,
With everything in my heart.

I have been here a long time.
Before I depart, I must
Account to You, for all I did
With my mortal dust.

The world was here before me.
It will remain after I have gone.
As on the Day of Creation
The Sun shines now as it shone.

The same earth and heaven
Were here in Adam's day;
Till the Day of Judgment,
Till Messiah comes they stay.

Lord God, Judge and Father,
Let my confession atone;
Forgive my secret transgressions,
Known to You and me alone.

Behold, my days are as hand breadths
My life of your spirit a breath.
Birth was my life's beginning.
Its end is death.

For my life, Lord, I thank You.
Now its end is near,
I confess to You all I remember,
Bend down, Lord, and hear.

All the dead were once living;
This earth they bestrode.
I pray, Lord, for Your forgiving,
When I join Your dead, Lord God.

The work of the dead is round us.
They built the streets we tread.
We eat fruit from trees they planted.
They wrote the books we read.

67

We pray to You, Lord, with the words
You taught them to pray.
We are laid down beside them.
Earth and dust as they.

If the earth were not here to receive me,
When my time comes to die,
Where would the earth from which You made me
Find its place, to lie?

As life is for the living,
Death is for the dead;
When all we had to do
Is consummated.

We join past generations;
My generation returns where it came.
We become one with Adam,
One with Abraham,

With our parents, friends and kindred,
Who before we died were dead;
Death brings us together,
Re-united.

Our dust returns to earth
Our spirit to You, Lord.
You will destroy death for ever,
According to Your Word.

We who sleep in the dust
Will praise you with jubilant cries.
Lord, command us to live,
That all the dead shall rise.

Lord, bend your ear
To the words I have said.
Raise me to live again,
Lord God who quickenest the dead.

POST MORTEM

"Lord God, I have come to you."
"You were always here."
"I was so far from you."
"I was always near."

"What lies in that wooden box?"
"Only your dead fear."
"Who speaks to you, now, Lord God?"
"You, who are here."